Original title:
Herb Garden Haikus

Copyright © 2025 Creative Arts Management OÜ
All rights reserved.

Author: Dexter Sullivan
ISBN HARDBACK: 978-1-80567-017-9
ISBN PAPERBACK: 978-1-80567-097-1

Nature's Aromatic Canvas

Basil dreams of pie,
Mint plots a leafy coup.
Rosemary brings the spice,
While parsley rolls a joint.

Thyme counts the minute,
Oregano's just lazy.
Sage whispers sweet nothings,
Chives snicker like kids.

Harmony in Herbal Hues

Cilantro wears its green,
Dill's dance is quite a sight.
Chervil just can't settle,
Lemongrass struts around.

Fennel's fronds are lofty,
Salvia rolls in laughter.
Bay leaves play a prank,
While tarragon just snores.

Serenade of the Stevia

Stevia sings sweet tunes,
Honey's having a fit.
Maple's in a flap,
Splenda's lost in thought.

Sugarcane can't keep up,
Molasses shakes her head.
Aspartame's too serious,
Sweet dreams on a vine.

Essence of the Earth

Lavender's in a twist,
Thyme lost track of time.
Oregano's giggles,
Herbs in a dance-off.

Basil joins the party,
Parsley takes a bow.
Each flavor in a whirl,
Sunshine in each leaf!

The Dance of Greenery

Basil winks in sun,
Sage does a little jig,
Oregano hums loud,
Mint twirls in the breeze.

Thyme slips on a leaf,
Rosemary shimmies bright,
Chives giggle and sway,
Parsley joins the fun.

Cilantro's a real tease,
Dancing 'til they drop,
Each green an artist,
They paint with their moves.

Lettuce makes a bow,
Carrots laugh, underground,
In this leafy groove,
The rhythm keeps them bound.

Palette of Nature's Bounty

In the soil they thrive,
Colors burst with each sprout,
Mint is quite the joker,
Parsley plays peek-a-boo.

Tomatoes blush with glee,
Peppers shout "Look at me!"
Zucchini twirls around,
While onions simply stare.

Charming herbs combine,
Creating quite a scene,
Dancing on the plate,
Flavors leap, fall, and tease.

Together they sing,
A funny little tune,
From soil to the dish,
Nature's jesters unite!

The Joy of Growing

Tiny seeds buried deep,
Dreaming of leafy greens.
I water them with hope,
And maybe a bit of beans.

Sunshine tickles their cheeks,
As they stretch towards the sky.
I peek through the petals,
To catch them waving 'Hi!'

Earth's Culinary Palette

Basil whispers gently,
'Add me to your stew!'
While cilantro confesses,
'I'm feeling bold too.'

Chives are joking around,
They think they're so cool.
But mint keeps insisting,
'Let's all jump in the pool!'

Seasons of Scent

Spring brings fresh rosemary,
Waving to the sun.
Summer's sweet sage giggles,
'Life's a spicy run!'

Autumn's thyme starts to dance,
In a swirling breeze.
Winter's parsley wonders,
'Am I lost in the freeze?'

Verdant Dreams

I dream of green treasures,
Dancing in my sleep.
Basil leads the parade,
While mint counts the sheep.

Gardening's a riddle,
With laughter and glee.
Each plant tells a story,
In this wild jubilee!

A Culinary Journey

Basil sneezes loud,
Thyme trips on a leaf,
Chives giggle and snicker,
Garlic breath disbelief.

Marjoram's on vacation,
Oregano's a clown,
Parsley sprinkles laughter,
As they tumble down.

The Heart of Flavor

Cilantro wears sunglasses,
Basil gets sunburned,
Parsley brings a picnic,
Mint just can't be turned.

Rosemary tells tall tales,
Thyme rolls on the floor,
While hot peppers wrestle,
Screaming, 'Bring some more!'

Gentle Whispers of Growth

Chives make silly faces,
Basil tries to sing,
Sage is on a mission,
To find the secret spring.

Thyme spins in circles,
Oregano's a tease,
Mint is dancing wildly,
Swaying in the breeze.

Potion of Flavor

Garlic brews a potion,
Herbs roam in delight,
Cooking up some magic,
Under stars so bright.

Parsley casts a spell,
Basil brews some cheer,
Each spoonful a secret,
Flavor's shift is near.

Moonlit Leaves

Under the pale moon,
Parsley dances with glee.
'I'm the star tonight!'
Said thyme with a smirk.

Chives in a tizzy,
Whispering sweet nothings.
'You think you're so cool?'
Lettuce rolls its eyes.

Sunshine and Spice

Basil basks in rays,
Planning its royal reign.
'I'll steal all your light!'
Sage chuckles nearby.

Mint joins the sun's fun,
Crafting minty delights.
'Try me in your tea!'
'Not too much!' warns Basil.

Nature's Hidden Spices

In the garden's heart,
Cilantro plots a scheme.
'I'll sneak into salsa!'
'Don't forget the lime!'

Oregano peeks through,
Saying, 'I spot a pizza!'
With a dash of flair,
Thyme adds a joke or two.

Vibrancy in the Soil

In the earth below,
Garlic dreams of a feast.
'I'll give them strong breath!'
Onion grins slyly.

Soil laughs and shakes hands,
'You all are quite the bunch!'
Together they thrive,
In this spicy joke fest.

Rosemary's Soft Embrace

Rosemary whispers,
"Breathe me in, dear friend!"
Rubbing thyme's shoulders,
They giggle and blend.

Sage wears a funny hat,
Chives twirl and sashay,
Oregano joins in,
It's a leafy ballet!

Elf-flavored Leaves

Tiny elves at play,
In the basil patch,
Mixing wild cocktails,
They dance and they hatch.

Mint brings the laughter,
With a peppermint grin,
While cilantro scolds them,
"Stop spitting my gin!"

Petals of Flavor

Petals bouncing around,
Dancing in the breeze,
"Try our new flavor!"
"It's sure to please!"

Chive flaunts its poise,
Like a king on parade,
While thyme rolls its eyes,
"Oh, please, give us shade!"

Garden Ink and Sea Salt

In the kitchen groove,
With spatulas bright,
Parsley writes recipes,
By candlelight.

Cilantro scoffs loud,
"My style's just the best!"
But all flavors agree,
"Together, we jest!"

Secrets of Basil

Whispers in the breeze,
Basil hides its secrets,
A leaf once sighed,
Now pesto dreams tonight.

Underneath the sun,
Basil flirts with the tomatoes,
A saucy romance,
In salad's secret world.

Dew-kissed Thyme

Morning dew giggles,
Thyme winks at sleeping bees,
They dance on petals,
In fragrant daydreams, wild.

A tiny little chef,
Seasoning dreams with laughter,
Thyme's a wise old sage,
In the kitchen's bustle.

Sage's Silent Song

Sage hums softly here,
Among pans and sizzling treats,
A culinary,
Secretive serenade.

In pots, it listens close,
To garlic's bold declarations,
Sage rolls its green eyes,
At thyme's boastful tales.

The Dance of Chives

Chives swish in the breeze,
Like dancers in a troupe,
Onions are too shy,
But chives shine and twirl.

With a wink, they prance,
Chopping jokes in the kitchen,
A snip and a giggle,
Chives rule the green stage.

Petals and Palate

I plucked a green sprout,
Ate it like a chip snack,
Flew into the sky,
Was grounded by the taste.

Greens wiggle and dance,
Flea beetles doing jazz,
My salad's a show,
The crunch steals the applause.

Fertile Ground's Lullaby

Earth snores softly now,
As seeds settle in cozy,
Caterpillars dream,
Waking with leafy plans.

Crickets play the drums,
While rabbits munch along,
"Dinner is served, folks!"
They sing their dinner song.

Roots That Inspire

Beneath the soil's coat,
Whispers of garlic's dreams,
"Plant me in some stew,"
It shouts from underground.

Radishes go rogue,
They think they own the bed,
"Who's the root now, huh?"
They tease the row above.

Seasons of the Herbal Bloom

Basil throws a bash,
Pesto fills the air thick,
Tomatoes crash in,
Salad dreams become real.

Mint dances on breeze,
In cocktails, it sways bright,
Sipping with a grin,
I swear the ice just winked.

Leaves of Wisdom

In the patch I stare,
Basil whispers secrets,
Thyme tells a joke,
And parsley just laughs.

Oregano's wild dance,
Mint twirls like a pro,
Sage brags of recipes,
That no one can bake.

Chives keep their cool,
While dill spins tales tall,
Rosemary's grumpy tale,
Of the time it got pruned.

In every green leaf,
A giggle, a sigh,
Nature's funny side,
Oh, how they do thrive.

Tiny Sprouts of Memory

Sprouts peek from the soil,
On a mission to grow,
They peek up and laugh,
At the weeds trying hard.

A tiny pepper's grin,
As big as my dream,
Radishes chuckle low,
While carrots play hide and seek.

In the sun's warm embrace,
Dill spins a tall tale,
Of garden adventures,
That made it a star.

With each sprout that pops,
A giggle is shared,
Nature's whimsy alive,
In the soil we adore.

Fragrance in the Breeze

Lemon balm whispers sweet,
Mint teases with a zest,
Rosemary's perfume,
Makes bees dance with joy.

Thyme sends out its scent,
Waving like a flag,
Sage strolls through the air,
Winking at the sun.

Lavender's soft hug,
Pops jokes in the breeze,
While chamomile sings,
A lullaby to green.

Oh, scents that can tickle,
And make your heart soar,
In this funny world,
Where smell is the score.

Garden Symphony in Bloom

In a maze of green,
The vines intertwine,
A chorus of giggles,
In every sweet leaf.

Basil strums a tune,
While thyme keeps the beat,
Chives hum in harmony,
The beetroot claps loud.

Flowering pep talks,
From carrots who care,
Every sprout's a note,
In this lush, leafy song.

Through the garden dance,
Laughter fills the air,
Nature plays the strings,
Of joy and delight.

Whispers of Basil

Basil's cheeky grin,
A leaf tickles my nose,
It whispers 'Add more,
I'm the king of your prose!'

In the salad, it hops,
Dancing on ripe tomatoes,
Singing, 'Look at me!
I'm the star of your flows!'

Noodles twirl in delight,
When basil joins the feast,
Saying with a wink,
'Your flavor's now increased!'

Oh, the pasta sighs,
As it spins 'round the bowl,
With basil's charm,
It steals the entire show!

Secrets in the Sage

Sage wears a wise hat,
Its leaves; soft and gray,
It mutters to the thyme,
'Let's spice up their day!'

Laughter in the breeze,
As it tickles the stew,
'The more we add in,
The tastier it's true!'

In the kitchen it lurks,
Knows all the right moves,
With a dash of charm,
It improves all our grooves!

Oh, sly little sage,
How you spice up our toast,
With each little pinch,
You're the flavor we boast!

Rosemary's Embrace

Rosemary's warm hug,
Wraps 'round my roasted dish,
'With me, you can't miss,
I'm your savory wish!'

It sleeps in the oven,
Dreaming of perfect fries,
Telling them sweet tales,
Of salt and sand that flies.

In a cake? Why not!
Rosemary knows no bounds,
With laughter and spice,
It turns life upside down!

So grab a sprig tight,
Let the flavor ignite,
This herb brings the fun,
In every single bite!

Thyme's Silent Dance

Thyme tiptoes around,
Whispers soft in the pot,
Joining culinary,
Where it's always a lot!

With every little sprig,
It shimmies with delight,
Turning plain to gourmet,
In the soft candlelight.

Perfect on a pizza,
Or in some soup divine,
Thyme dances with joy,
In each culinary line!

Oh, sly little thyme,
With a laugh and a wink,
You're the life of the dish,
Making us all think!

Rhythms of the Rain-Bound Roots

Droplets dance on leaves,
A puddle's a mirror,
Where snails throw a soirée,
And worms lead the line.

The basil sings in glee,
As thunderstorms do roll,
But mint thinks it's a joke,
With a giggle and twirl.

Thyme tells tales of rain,
While the soil hums along,
But parsley jumps in fear,
At the squawking of crows.

When sun peers through clouds,
The garden throws a bash,
Sunchoke and beet root dance,
To a breeze, full of cheer.

Colorful Harvests in the Dawn

Dawn sprinkles confetti,
As peppers put on shoes,
Radishes roll their eyes,
A tomato's too shy.

Lettuce in a tutu,
Spins with the morning sun,
While chives are all gossip,
On the latest dirt score.

Cabbage waves its green flag,
Join the veggie parade,
With carrots in a cart,
They make such a scene!

At dusk, they all settle,
In the garden of dreams,
Constellations of plants,
Cheerfully whispering.

Whispers of Green

In a forest of green,
The dill has a crush,
While the sage plays it cool,
And the chives giggle hard.

'What a wild romance!'
Cries coriander with glee,
As thyme makes a pun,
On the love in the breeze.

A sprout takes a selfie,
While onions roll their eyes,
And beet root pulls faces,
At the kale's awkward stance.

In this playful patch,
Nature's silly affair,
All laugh at the rain,
And the sun's beaming glare.

Nature's Aromatic Canvas

A splash of bold aromas,
In a canvas of green,
Rosemary paints with flair,
While parsley dabs with ease.

'Is that me or the thyme?'
Oregano winks sly,
While the fennel snickers,
At the antics around.

Basil wears a beret,
As he curates the taste,
Ginger rolls out the laughs,
In this quirky bouquet.

Lavender's in a mood,
With giggles of lemon,
This garden of laughter,
Is a feast for the senses.

Tonic of the Earth

Worms gossip below,
They're plotting lettuce wins,
Parsley eavesdrops close,
A salad world begins.

Earthworms kiss the soil,
Chard giggles in the sun,
Kale flexes its greens,
Fitness for everyone!

Tomatoes roll in line,
Dancing with the breeze,
Basil dreams of pasta,
Life's a slice of cheese!

Serenade to Cilantro

Cilantro claims the stage,
Shaking off the haters,
Its scent throwing shade,
To bland, non-flavor traitors.

Chop it fine, it sings,
Guacamole's best mate,
A green confetti,
Spicing up the plate!

"Stop!" the coriander cries,
"Not everyone will cheer!"
It holds its fresh bouquet,
And winks, "I'll persevere!"

Raindrops on Green

Raindrops tickle leaves,
A dance of tiny stars,
Basil wears a crown,
Looking quite like a czar.

Dill rolls down the stem,
In puddles, thyme does float,
Oregano splashes,
In this herb-y boat.

Lettuce hums with glee,
As droplets join the show,
Together they sing,
Nature's own water flow!

Murmurs of Mint

Mint whispers to sage,
"Let's throw a garden bash!"
"Invite thyme and rosemary,
We'll mix it up in a flash!"

Cocktail dreams abound,
With mojitos galore,
Mint twirls in the sun,
Begging for one drink more.

Even chives pop in,
Their laughs reach the sky,
"Herb up, folks, join in!"
As summer rolls by.

Clover's Untold Stories

In a patch of green,
Leprechauns hide their gold,
Tales that tickle toes,
And giggles take their hold.

Dandelions dance,
With fluff that sings in the breeze,
Whispers of mischief,
Beneath the sneaky trees.

Mice wear tiny hats,
As they throw a picnic feast,
Crumbs that fly and flop,
An unexpected beast!

Grasshoppers gossip,
Over tea brewed from salt air,
Swaying in the sun,
With stories they all share.

Roots of Serenity

Carrots wear cool shades,
Rooted deep in mellow earth,
Learning from the peas,
Life's lessons of pure mirth.

Radishes are shy,
In a coat of spicy red,
Peeking from the dirt,
With laughter in their head.

Beets compete in sports,
Rolling races down the lane,
With tops held so high,
They stride to claim their fame.

Turnips throw a party,
In the moonlight's soft embrace,
Grooves of glee abound,
Let loose in earthy space.

Echoes of an Edible Meadow

Tomatoes with a grin,
Bursting with a juicy laugh,
Picnics in the sun,
Nature's funny photograph.

Basil wears a cape,
Hero of the flavor game,
He saves spaghetti,
From tasting quite the same.

Oregano sings out,
To the tune of garlic's toast,
Together they dance,
A culinary boast.

Lettuce spins and twirls,
In their crisp and crunchy way,
Salad bowl of joy,
Mixing laughter at the play.

The Scent of Growth

Minted magic swirls,
In the air, a playful tease,
Bees buzz with a grin,
As they dance among the leaves.

Chives are giggling loud,
With a taste so fresh and bright,
Swirling in the breeze,
Adding joy to every bite.

Thyme's a sneaky one,
Whispers secrets to the sage,
Growing side by side,
In this earthy mini stage.

Parsley throws confetti,
At the festival of beats,
Freshness all around,
And food that can't be beat!

Taste of the Sun's Embrace

Basil wears sunglasses,
Mint is sipping iced tea,
Thyme cracks a bad joke,
Laughter spills like honey.

Chives dance in the breeze,
Parsley pranks the tomatoes,
Rosemary chimes in,
Sage rolls her eyes, "Oh, no!"

Sun-kissed leaves giggle,
Bees buzz in delight,
Carrots tell wild tales,
Of roots deep in the night.

All together we sing,
Nature's joyful feast,
Fruits of sun's embrace,
Who knew veggies could be beasts?

Fragrant Shadows

Cilantro's in the shade,
Lemon balm let out a cough,
Oregano slips jokes,
And rosemary just scoffs.

In the twilight hour,
Thyme starts a funny tale,
Basil's got the giggles,
As mint begins to wail.

Parsley tries to dance,
But tangled in the vines,
Chives can hardly breathe,
From laughing 'bout their lines.

Their fragrant shadows play,
A comedic ballet,
In the garden's laughter,
Where even weeds can sway.

Kaleidoscope of Greens

Spinach flips a coin,
Dill debates its bold fate,
Arugula pranks hard,
With a peppery rate.

Cabbage wears a crown,
Kale struts down the lane,
Lettuce cracks a smile,
In the crisp, leafy game.

Chard shows all its colors,
Green in every hue,
Herbs throw a big bash,
With laughs and a stew!

Basil runs a race,
To win the salad prize,
In this patch of joy,
Surprise with each green rise!

Twilight in the Herb Patch

Night falls with a wink,
Mint hums a silly tune,
Thyme slinks to the beat,
While shadows grow too soon.

Basil shares his dreams,
Of pasta and a dance,
Chives twirl in delight,
In a green, merry trance.

Moonlight bathes the patch,
A serenade of scents,
Basil asks for ice cream,
While parsley just laments.

As stars join the fun,
The herbs laugh and play,
In the twilight glow,
Sunset marks their day!

Lavender Dreams Under Moonlight

In twilight's soft glow,
Lavender whispers sweet dreams,
Bugs dance in moonlight,
Wishing for honeyed beams.

Scented pillows of bliss,
Bees snore in fragrant beds,
A lavender tease,
Tickles the silly heads.

Steeped in night's magic,
Chasing away all the blues,
Fields of velvet shades,
In pajamas made of dew.

With dreams wrapped in silk,
Laughter blooms in the hush,
Under stars that wink,
We giggle and softly blush.

Minted Moments in the Breeze

Mint sprigs sway and twist,
A refreshing little tease,
Breeze whispers secrets,
Of mojitos and sweet leaves.

Sipping on laughter,
Mint tea spills zephyrs bright,
Worms wear tiny hats,
While ants groove with delight.

Pouncing green intruders,
In our cooler's domain,
Minty mischief blooms,
As they sip on our grain.

Chasing after scents,
We shuffle in glee tonight,
With mint on our breath,
And the world feeling right.

Cilantro's Fresh Awakening

Cilantro wakes up,
With a grin on green leaves,
A guacamole dance,
That the avocado weaves.

Tacos jump for joy,
Dancing on sizzling plates,
Cilantro, the queen,
Of spicy dinner fates.

Pesto on the rise,
Basil's older cousin fights,
With cumin and lime,
For taste bud heights and flights.

Waving at the sun,
With flavors wild and free,
Cilantro shouts loud,
"Come gymnastic with me!"

The Echo of Oregano

Oregano shouts bold,
As pizza joins the fun,
A sprinkle of magic,
Dances 'round like the sun.

Sweater weather vibes,
Mushrooms in cozy hugs,
Stories simmer low,
As the pot toots and shrugs.

Underneath the stars,
Oregano takes a bow,
Inviting all the folks,
To enjoy a big chow.

With laughter spiced bright,
We feast till we can't move,
Echoes of oregano,
In flavors that groove.

In the Shade of Parsley

Green garnishes sway,
A sneaky cat rolls by,
Parsley whispers low,
"Don't eat me, oh my!"

The chives gossip loud,
About the basil's charm,
They all want the crown,
Plant gossip's quite the harm!

Cilantro's a thrill,
Salsa justice at stake,
Tomatoes conspire,
A tasty mistake!

Onions hide their tears,
Laughing from the side,
"We'll crop up just fine,
We've got nothing to hide!"

Nature's Zesty Palette

Thyme's a little sly,
Sneaking in some thyme jokes,
"Why did the basil,
Join us? It's a hoax!"

Paintbrush of bright greens,
Each pot a piece of art,
Pesto dreams abound,
With flavors that start!

Oregano hums low,
In the summer's heat,
"Hope you like my spice,
And my dance with feet!"

Dill is quite ideal,
With a pickle in hand,
Chortles of delight,
In this savory land!

Sun-kissed Lavender

Lavender's soft jokes,
Float above the dew,
"Why are bees so sweet?
I've always liked their view!"

With sunflowers they laugh,
In a twirl of gold,
"We're the real rocket,
Just watch our stories unfold!"

Scented misty dreams,
Hang in the warm breeze,
While rosemary strays,
Rustling like it flees.

In the evening hours,
They sip chamomile tea,
Sharing spicy tales,
Of zest and jubilee!

A Symphony of Sprouts

Sprouts hum a sweet tune,
In their tiny green caps,
Radishes keep beat,
With their little taps!

Peas play the maracas,
As carrots cut loose,
While lettuce wave hands,
In an organized moose!

Spinach sings of strength,
Flipping leaves with flair,
Bok choy leads the dance,
Everyone has a pair!

Chard joins the ballet,
In a vibrant pirouette,
This garden's a show,
With flavors to bet!

Tiny Petals and Tall Tales

Tiny blooms so bright,
Came to play in the sun,
Whispering secrets,
Of the best bug that won.

Dancing with the bees,
Tickled by soft breezes,
Little comrades laugh,
In their joyous frolics.

A squirrel once claimed,
This patch belongs to me,
But the mint said, "No way!"
"We're all here, you see!"

Laughter in the air,
As the critters convene,
Together they know,
Life's a silly scene.

Aroma of the Anise

Anise left a trail,
Of sweetness on the path,
A cat took a whiff,
And started doing math.

She measured the stars,
With a whisker and paw,
Declared, "This is fun!"
"I'll be in the next draw!"

With flavors so bold,
The spice made her dance,
Twisting and turning,
In a fragrant trance.

All the critters cheered,
As they joined her parade,
Who knew that anise,
Had this fun escapade?

Green Fingers and Soft Shadows

Green fingers at play,
Planting seeds in the dirt,
One sprout said to me,
"Hey, this tickles my skirt!"

A robin flew down,
To critique the décor,
Said, "Chic isn't here,
Let's not plant anymore!"

The shadows grew long,
As the sun waved goodbye,
A snail took a leap,
And forgot how to fly.

With laughter all around,
In the soft evening light,
The garden sang songs,
Of the comical night.

Beneath the Herbaceous Canopy

Under leafy green,
A pickle tells a tale,
Of a wayward cucumber,
Who went off the rail.

"I swear I was plucked,
For a moment in fame,
But ended in relish,
What a culinary shame!"

The parsley just snickered,
At the pickle's grand plight,
"At least you're not toast,
You're still holding on tight!"

Chives giggled and swayed,
Underneath the soft shade,
In the herbaceous scene,
All the joy they had made.

Shimmering Petals

Bees dancing in air,
Lavender's sweet embrace,
She tried to catch one,
Now it's a buzzing race!

Mint leaves in a stew,
Silly chef slips and slides,
He claimed it was art,
But his pride he now hides!

Chives laugh in the breeze,
Whispering secret jokes,
Garlic's breath nearby,
Makes everyone choke!

Oregano's bright flair,
Dancing on sunny days,
With pizzazz they twirl,
In their green laugh-filled ways.

Earth's Perfumed Palette

Rosemary's sly grin,
Stealing thyme's fancy clothes,
Summer's prankster vibes,
In this patch, laughter grows!

Sage and basil brawl,
Over the sunny spot,
One claims it's his throne,
While the other just hot!

Cilantro's fresh wink,
Confusing some palates,
It just wants to be,
In all the best salads!

Parsley's dancing hat,
Waving at the sun,
Each leaf a delight,
Nature's silly fun!

Gentle Caress of the Wind

Wind whispers to thyme,
"Let's take a little ride!"
He chuckles with flair,
And the chives open wide!

Lettuce gets a chill,
In its cool leafy dress,
"I'm not going out!"
But it's a funny mess!

Dill rolls down the path,
Bouncing with every gust,
First a leaf, then laughs,
Now it's just plain rust!

Fennel twirls around,
Pretending it's a star,
Show off that green frock,
Oh, what a bizarre!

Spirals of Thrift

Thyme curls up in spirals,
Dreams of becoming tea,
But each time it brews,
It just tickles me!

Basil's fancy shoes,
He wears them with pure pride,
Trip over themselves,
On that fresh herb slide!

Scented vines in winks,
Spreading laughter in sun,
Even rosemary,
Joined the silly fun!

Camomile's quiet smirk,
"Just brew me!" it will call,
But every sip of cheer,
Makes you giggle and fall!

Symphony in the Soil

Worms dance in delight,
Twirling under the sun,
Beets hum a sweet tune,
While carrots sneak a pun.

Basil dreams of pizza,
Thyme plots a savory plot,
Mint revels in frolic,
Parsley gets the last shot.

Sage sings of old tales,
A chorus of green leaves,
Each note a fresh flavor,
As nature gently cleaves.

In this dirt-coated band,
Happiness sprouts and sways,
With laughter in the air,
A silly herb-filled play.

Ode to Green Ambrosia

Chives wear tiny hats,
Ready for a tea party,
Cilantro brings confetti,
And dill is quite the smarty.

Oregano's a joker,
Telling thyme-filled jokes,
While rosemary just giggles,
As minty banter pokes.

This spice cabinet fest,
Of flavors we adore,
Brings joy to our dishes,
And laughter to encore.

So raise a toast to greens,
For they bring bliss and cheer,
A funny brew of taste,
In nature's grand frontier.

Aromatic Epiphanies

Cilantro sneezes spice,
While parsley takes a breath,
Lavender whispers dreams,
Of scents that conquer death.

Thyme's clock is always ticked,
As basil tells a lie,
Mint sips on cool water,
And causes quite a sigh.

Oregano paints skies,
With shades of savory zest,
Each bloom brings forth a laugh,
In this fragrant little fest.

So gather 'round the plot,
For wit and flavors blend,
Aromatic giggles thrive,
In this garden we defend.

Garden of Tastes

In dirt our flavors grow,
Each sprout a chuckle found,
Kale jokes in the breeze,
While spinach spins around.

Sweet peas play a prank,
As beans climb up the wall,
Radishes toss puns,
While cabbage starts to call.

Fennel dreams of candy,
While leeks compose a tune,
Each note a taste sensation,
Underneath the moon.

This plot of silly joy,
With laughter on a plate,
In our garden of tastes,
Eating never feels late.

The Language of Leaves

Chives gossip at dawn,
Whispers of savory plans.
Mint teases the night sky,
'Time to sip my sweet tea!'

Thyme talks in riddles,
Sage sighs in deep thoughts.
Basil brings the chaos,
'Who stole my spicy socks?'

Wandering through my patch,
Cilantro grins with glee.
Parsley rolls its eyes,
'Why are herbs so chatty?'

Oregano plays tricks,
Popping up uninvited.
'I'll spice up your curry!'
But only when you're tired.

Scented Reverie

Rosemary dreams in green,
Sharing thoughts with the bees.
Oregano's a prankster,
'Just check your lunchbox, please!'

Parsley brings the laughter,
Saying 'Life's a green show!'
Mint jumps out in costume,
'Who wants a minty glow?'

Basil claims the spotlight,
In a sombrero made of thyme.
'Join our spicy salsa,
It's guaranteed to rhyme!'

Cilantro's green mustache,
Dangles as it winks.
'Watch me dance in the breeze,
With all these fragrant clinks!'

Threshold of the Wild

At the edge of my plot,
Lemongrass waves hello.
'Adventure's waiting here,
Let's find where wild things grow!'

Basil rides a butterfly,
Chamomile writes a book.
Cilantro's doing yoga,
'Just see my leafy look!'

Tarragon climbs a fence,
Wondering what's outside.
'Is that parsley in disguise?
Or just a leafy ride?'

Thyme plays hide and seek,
While dill takes a peek too.
'Watch for backyard giants!
I hear they love a stew!'

Enchanted Flora

In the glow of twilight,
Mint summons moonbeam friends.
Lemongrass starts a dance,
Basil brings the new trends.

Rosemary winks with flair,
Sage sends a loving hug.
'Join our secret party,
On a big cozy rug!'

Cilantro's DJing now,
With a green, leafy beat.
'Let's spin this veggie fresh,
And shake those dance floor feet!'

Thyme makes silly hats,
Decorated with zest.
'Under stars we'll party,
In our leafy nest!'

Parsley's Green Medley

Parsley in the breeze,
Dancing with the tomatoes,
Twirls and little leaps,
Kicking up soil, oh please!

Silly leaves so bright,
Splashing green in my stew,
Who knew you could play?
Parsley, you're quite the sight!

Basil shouts, "Not fair!"
While thyme rolls on the ground,
"I'm just here to taste!"
Herb gossip all around!

Together they enjoy,
A green medley of cheer,
We laugh, we add spice,
The best of friends, oh dear!

Dill's Gentle Caress

Dill dives into pickles,
Wishing for a crunchy bite,
Hugs the cucumbers tight,
Whispering, "You're my pickle!"

In the salad bowl,
Dill wears a zesty hat,
Says, "I'm a big deal!"
While everyone stares at that.

Turns out dill's a tease,
Winking at the mustard,
"Join my game, I swear!"
Humor's never lost, absurd!

In sandwiches so stacked,
Dill finds a cozy spot,
Jokes shared with each bite,
This is the life, I thought!

Chive's Whispered Wishes

Chives in the corner,
Hatching tiny dreams,
"How tall can I grow?"
Sprouting with little beams.

Waving at the peas,
"Hey, don't you look nice!"
A chive will always try,
To spread joy and entice!

Chives play peek-a-boo,
With flowers all around,
Plant gossip circulates,
Quiet snickers abound.

In cooking, they prance,
Garnishing with flair,
Chives' whispered wishes,
Are heard everywhere!

A Symphony of Scents

Scented leaves collide,
In a fragrant ballet,
Garlic, rosemary,
All dancing away!

Basil hums a tune,
Sage keeps up the beat,
Oregano claps hands,
As they twirl on their feet.

Thyme's antics are cute,
While mint plays the flute,
Lavender sings sweetly,
A joke none can refute.

Together they sway,
In this theater of smells,
Each note brings a laugh,
In this garden, all's well!

www.ingramcontent.com/pod-product-compliance
Lightning Source LLC
Chambersburg PA
CBHW072140200426
43209CB00051B/192